Penny Marvel
& the book of the city
of selfys

DUSIE | dusie.org

ISBN: 978-1-944253-06-6
LCCN: 2018943578

Penny Marvel & the book of the city of selfys

Elizabeth Treadwell

The cartography of the soul is not abstract. It is drawn
painstakingly and specifically by direct experience.
Arielle Guy

The key is in remembering, in what is chosen for the dream. In the
silence of recovery we hold the rituals of the dawn, now as then.
Paula Gunn Allen

Penny Marvel & the book of the city of selfys

Book One
Narnia

What Happened at the Front Door
[draft Narnia selfy no. 4]

... bearers translating, arriving notorious
as a girl's name, a pet form; feeding on
grasses, plants, leaves, and bark;
the pressing of words into dreams—

the terror of charm

her long hair,
her mercy

as the characters shift,
all of their own accord,
& the stars—

*there must be worlds you could get to through every pool in the
wood*

there was soon enough light for them to see one another's faces

Reception
[draft Narnia selfy no. 9]

our hearts dark & tiny
swans, falling from
a twisting crescent
moon

Then came a sound even more delicious than the sound of water.

Lawn
[draft Narnia selfy no. 14]

and after that was
a room all hung with
green; with a harp in
one corner

her outer mantle
joyously

    discarded,
    some very

stone mouths
    pitch paws / elated

the bevelled decanters of our glowing faith

Shore
[draft Narnia selfy no. 25]

even some of the trees are on her side

while you were
i held

the seashells to my ears
clothed in the mantle
of my own desiring

and while i
u did
the same

everybodie's souls
of the new gold earth
in which energie

into the singing fields
into our bodies of chalk

Veil
[draft Narnia selfy no. 32]

getting to corpse
the sea, the blood, the taffy
birds & light, horizon

& all our glowing coverings
our skins/our bones
our bones

*Then imagine instead of the black or gray or chestnut back of the
horse the soft roughness of golden fur, and the mane flying back in
the wind.*

Wood
[draft Narnia selfy no. 46]

aqua, celandine, drab
northern trees, our living
works & ministrations

we champion each other

                    we couldn't sleep

their small foldy wings, the children

all the human things, paths & objects

our palms/our palms

Book Two

Solarpunk
or selfy as the final burden of
consciousness wrecked by sea-wave

god

god,

borne in the remnants
of your fat scum

Leda

even as the moon
carried our earthly griefs

Aphrodite, or selfy as the sound of Venus

informed by salt & light
the crystalline
remembrances & membranes
all the pretty selfys of the seas

hero, or selfy as chance crowning a sleeping man
[selfy after Mina Loy]

the bitterlies contested
not the flow
this dream is a tablet of light
its shadows very close

Artemis [reprise] [or selfy after
William Carlos Williams]

all the bald anthems
in our sugarginger cars
as we sought our purchased highs
those mighty raring heraldries
throwing stones for our besties
for all our pious thieves & showmen
all up in the drifty fabrics of these seas
as the elements sing as we placate
information, our wounds alert
& tearing, our arrows echoing

Christine & Justice

smack dab in the wreck and the beauty
to give birth to
opaque water-based
imaginaries of the dawn
in the hand-sewn novitiate
in the hand-carved light
along the golden borders and the tender roofs
the sun's blaze and its caress
our chalk bodies in silverlilt
into this darkened night
into the palace of our inevitable
into the singing fields
smack dab in the wreck and the beauty
all we tossed into our landscape avoidant
sacked in its vault of angels
there's a handmade border
a hut on stilts astride the shore
the oldest portrait of our
heroine and hero
its courtyard parapet
its air and flooring, rickety
its underdrawing, seam
its nourishments, its actions
of our own becoming
in the hand-sewn
in the hand-carved light
in the silver apparel of our communion
embroideries and opaque
smack dab

Athena, or selfy as Woman protecting a unicorn
from a hunter

my mind is flooded with tenderness
my tendons, my wrists, my chalkish bones

& my womb
blooms with this

selfy as the duchess of normcore

the gnostics give birth to him again and again,
forever normcore, in the sacred cave of
subjectivity and wife-ish splendor, whereby
doctrine cauldron inhale
oak damsels magpie entrail—
the nymph echo
as the fish
and the rivers
cry

i am a broken human
trying to be good

selfy as Mary Magdalen as a hermit

maydenys dignite, as in
our light

the weary beast
a still and private thing
among the sages

penny magdalen

the girls in their brave dresses
with their sweet penny hands
seeking a magdalen alcove
a repository for their unbidden prayers

Andromeda selfy

in these fur seas
our brighty faces
waving from the greeny shallows

in these fur seas
our ginger crowns

such lacy bright impresses
along the sun & fate

in the lavender mysteries
our dream skies
& quiet wakings

Pip

in the johnny seed, such visions
pool & flare
the ravening sibilants
slide into darkbright
cherry petals
drop in herds
upon the wetted pavements

in the johnny seed, our tender roofs & portraits
witness key & elk, witness
the stomachs of the books,
an anterior yellow,
buttered in time,
furred in herds

these words
please come

The Weary Beasty

33

i am still a cowed sea-bird,
timiding the water;
even as i crow about.
to be the coveted & despised
thing, orlando,
the buffalo murdered along
the rails the men in ceaseless
splendor.
it is wearying, fernanda,
i write you from my
scared sea cave
scarred in weather,
clowned in form's decree
still/living

still living at the scarred sea-cave
with legs, and heart, in earthen.

lord

you mayn't prey, lord
lord, you mayn't prey

in the outrageous factory, sirs
we are declining

Penserosa: a novitiate

we are each the source
of our own novitiate

in the hand-sewn
in the hand-carved light
of our own becoming

our chalk bodies
our palms our bones

wearing our fathers faces
clothed in our mothers gowns of flesh

to stand before you
unadorned

selfy as Penelope, & measures

the twins the drafts the works

in undulary confessory
bird, pin, note

cry myth
as this thin azure

along love's queer flame

selfy as the final burden of consciousness wrecked by sea-wave

Solarpunk

covered in ashes
we tremble & stir
cloaked in voices
we listen & tend

Oh in & of the dark, song-mother, the seas, the skies,
the landings. beings, creatures, amplitudes. each sharp-
shouldered radiance, every mecca, each shoreline
its shell-gate.

Book Three
Holocene

sweet barbizons,
        vulnerary & scenes—

sweet barbizons,
        the tvs & the fires—

resemblance

toward our salt house
the dark ink washes me
the flecks of pebbled light

my body is the sea the sea
my body is
the sea

[hers] [iterations]

as we linger in this copse-place
our shadows & our bearings & our light
first narrows, then scenes
in all our lambly heraldry, holocene,
remembrances & membranes

portaling

we wear no hesitation amid this star-dark night
this dawn & this twilight, the smooth
impermanence of men, so rocky & so free,
our chalk bodies near the seas
sky-bright accounting, newish world
what fringed beings are we now

hill-song for Julie

mountaineering into story, which pours toward us
as we lay down our tools & valor
softly eating, recalling those visionary girls
of history & selfy, of jessamy fertility

mountaineering into story, which pours toward us
as we lay down our tools & valor
tell of our lives as matrons
in the swimmy tides of rain-soaked pavements
in our fortunes & our shoes

the forgiveness of our sins our sorrows
historical already
under a neighbor sky

lake-song for Holly

at the place of the lake-oak
we pour our dreams our methods
we anchor each other
draw down starlight
draw down all our fresh arcana

we linger at this copse-place
verify these meadowed hours

as the geese, they flap & nibble

in all this earthen shapeliness
tidal, & forlorn, an inlet, sanctuary

as our children grow
so tall beside us
they run to us & tell us
of all their fresh arcana

at the place of the lake-oak
at the place of
all our fresh arcana

we anchor each other
draw down starlight to see
each other's faces

we linger at this copse-place
we pour our dreams our methods
as the geese, they watch & beg

of all our fresh arcana
draw down starlight in breathing
mend ourselves & trees

as our children grow
so tall beside us
they run to us & tell us
they curl & they witness
they witness & they curl

draw down starlight
pour their dreams their methods
like carpets to the sea

as the geese they silently

an inlet, herald sea
our spirits float & soar there
our bodies are the sea
the sea our bodies are
the sea

for we are made
of dark & salt
of waterlight
of care of care
of care

for we are made
of dark & salt
of waterlight
of care of care
of care

as into the herald sea
we anchor each other
draw down starlight to see
each other's faces

at the curvy lake-oak
the inlet & the copse-place

our starry breath the sea
our love it pours
right through our cells
our love
it does not end

the lake & its perimeter
star-bright & very close
here we house each other
like heralds to the sea

as the geese they flap & nibble
as our shadows & our bearings & our light

as our shadows & our bearings & our light
as our love it pours
right through our cells
as our love it does not end

& here
the dark ink washes me
the flecks of pebbled light

our bodies are the sea the sea
our bodies are the sea
for we are made
of dark & salt
of waterlight
of care of care
of care
for we are made
of dark & salt
of waterlight
of care of care
of care

in loving memory of my friend Holly Schneider

sweet barbizons, the tvs & the fires

our rough old sun
so bright for us

our stems, our crowns, our bones

in vocabularies hollows, my beloved reticence

the sanctuary at belpine

a vessel & a crown,
bee ointment,
candlelight, blossom,
an ear, a parchment, a perfume
embodied memory
a homemade scepter
the constant magic
of their offerings

intention for the pink moon (aperture)

your small eyes my angels
our bodies heavens anchors

a penny drafty

in memory's wild mercy
such drifty amblers are we
wearing our masks and our sleeves

as our eyes leak earthen footsongs
leak our trellised hymns
in kind teeth, amid the shores

seeking the wound's remedy
sorting the mary chairs
of heartbeat's solemn claim

as we bathe and clothe and ache
our windy ornamentals
our beribboned pantheons

such drifty amblers are we
as we resemble
the chorused patterns

the unkempt courage
of the stars
in the hand-held mercy

of all our sweet red summers, blessingbirds
our ancient mannequins
of the coming light

of hollows (drafting)

yes all women
injurious as dust

of our sharp rock
of spinning into
skies to waters

our rough old sun
so bright for us
so beastly

sweet barbizons,
the tvs & the fires

the private diaries of the saints
the beloved maturities of the women

the fairly cwen, her blousy robes & pinny hairdo
her library of gown & story, trestled
we, novitiate, devour it

small cardboard boxes
stamped in othertime, parting at the seams
house sheets & drafts & booklets

excitedly, as she, an old woman, allows us
we, a young group of young girls,
grab & carry, mend & wear

our heart's recompense, our inheritance
of feminine wonder, & thus we balcony
against a possible night sky

now, the inquisition is fini, yo
by the lake-oak
in the copse-place

as narrations lonely gut parlor
births, unprincipled, unmastered,
a new economy of light

of light, epic & herald, brilliant & kind — & kindred —

foul-mouthed, besotted, real

to come into being
against a dark
against a possible night sky

to rest & to wake & to stir
like coral from a red
a deep sea bed

to draw sustenance to be received
housed in marrow, pulse & voice
to sense, to part

to part, to sense, to unveil
to portal & to nurse, to turn
our airs, our bones, our teeth, our milk

in these fur seas
our ginger crowns
such lacy bright impresses
along the sun & fate

to be held, food-heavy
sweet barbizons

our figures shaped
of dark & salt
of waterlight
of care
of care
of care

yes all women, dear vastlies, sisterbels
brotherbirds, stargazies, twins
our bright odd being, buttercups, sweet barbizons,
the vulnerary & the scenes

sweet mother, mouth, & murmur
sweet father, daughter, son, & well
yes all beings, yes tenderly clefts & hollows
dear mountains, cities, shores, & stems

impervious as dust
on our sharp rock
of spinning into
skies & waters

our bright old sun
so rough for us
our counsel

Sophiakin

of the Sophia fields
under the Mary tree
all the little girls named Sophia
run and dance
play amid the tall swooshy grasses
and in the nubbly glens
collect rocks
assemble their symbols
and ways

Sophia Jean assembles
Sophia Rae assembles
Sophia Marie assembles
Sophia Grace assembles
Sophiakin assembles
Sophiabel assembles
all the little girls named Sophia

Sophia Joan
Sophia Reina
Sophia Victoria
Sophia Veronica
Sophia Valentina
Sophia Alma
Sophia Maria
Sophia
all the little girls named Sophia

late dynasty statuette   59

in clerestory antiphon
let angels hug your theory head
and paint your sugar nails

tiara

cool us to shafts
with just
the mother rhymes
the riddles

charming the lessons
into the cures

in our wintergreen anchorite garment
shedding skins like a loose rind

diana at the edge world
for AG

arrows drawn & arrows pierced
anchorite moonshine
in this vast, precessional star turn
the silken flames & the milky
sustenance of the shades

our palms
filled on fruit there
in these undergrowth
our breath's canopy
our stories are here
awash in this
evaporative,
bony

the idillio of persephone triumphant
for KW

in the quiet fields of our discernment
in the dense glens of our loneliness
along the shoreline
the marrow of our home
the wild solace
of you

sweet barbizons,
          the tvs & the fires—

this sainted reckoning

these holocene

in ancient witness, barbizon

in the cleft love

press your wounds to mine
our sacred injurie

diaphany

it is ornately sewn
in all the herald portraits
of the seas

our bodies are the seas
the seas
our bodies are
the seas

Book Four

odes in earthen reverdie, & Marys

The iron in your blood comes from the instant before a star
dies....you cut yourself and you see that red from that
oxygenated hemoglobin....and that was the instant of the
death of a solar system...   *Michelle Thaller, NASA*

at the temple
amid the soil
of love's transfiguring
we are all clergy now

fleck

Venus in the palms
as Lilith admits her devotion
and Eve rescinds her rule
as out of their wild purses
in this dense formulaics eventide
their reptilian familiars
purr-purr

fractal

it is our bright fate
this fluency, this wobble
as into the wild keep

Jesus or the phenomena of aldermen

in your creche hands
the physical preventatives, scour
our twinned inventions of press & flow
ashing myself with mud & mercy
money as a phrase, an atmosphere
some pretty science, a feather in the air
in dashing spells intoxicants
& by the wild seas

[&]

& all the species trembled
as the stars sang above us
& the trees returned our sighs

Philae

affection being named the daughter
of discernment, the diminutive
of a rose which is a rose
floating in a meadow in the window
of a shop, in a spiral, long ago,
thorny and still, as the words bunch
toward eternity

Lunar

as our faces grow more intricate
in the wind, the blaze, the flood
the rich pile of narration
like the flounce and flurry of our skirts
bequeaths us, nurse, and slave, and witch
dissolves & hollows from our centers the milky magic
of the way, which we birth and reach for
and caress, in earthling sustenance
mud caked star bright leaf breathed
as we move along these shores

Lilith

in this world of flesh & candor
we aren't all alone

Land-doll

I wait at the door/to eternity/because you mean/that much to me
—The Gogos

1. Mortar

as into the unwitting/shrine fatigue
we pour, oh skinbox
of my heart, for access to your quickest place
my love unaltering

2. Bridge

these days are huge & gallant
milk-heralds of the deeps
the production fatigues of the land-dolls
of all the human creep, in fantasia, and lab,
go soft, go gently now, let us weep,
witness flares & circulation
all the gear & all the battles shed
go soft, go gently now, let us weep,
barefooted, sunk to floor

3\. Vermillion, or two women in vermillion light
(after Elmer Bischoff)

found in mammals & associated with the process of blood clotting —
Webster's New Universal Unabridged Dictionary (Dorset & Baber,
1955 & 1983)

any of a certain round
or oval disks, sat up in the mending-
place, the garments worn & common
hollow, as the light haloes a tracery, unchambered
a sky-shroud path borne round the privies,
touched & grazed & crowned in stars,
& nursing

Querent

guys, how bout we hate technology, in the game?
curse you, airplane! —Gemma Jackson

love like a river mark soul after soul, faulty linguist
in sorrowful data, our radiance
& our regal dusk, for we are of the mary bones,
still sparkling with her breathing & we
are of ourselves awakened

Book Five
Manual of devotions

BAMBINA SULLA PORTA [after Felice Carena]

for we are made
of pine & ash,
the abandoned lighthostels
of a world once known
as we climb
into our voices,
flesh & breath

[*]

these worlds created at
our sites of mending
& of acute recompense
materials & valence, mercy-tide,
ev'ry sundry of threshold & again of clime
in unison, & sugar,
parliament—

DEL VALLE BY REQUEST
[with Ivy, Gemma, Muriel, Sofia, Isabel & Kailamae]

there's magic held in rocks & grasses
the green flowing of the stream
polliwogs & winds through branches
girls in their gathering
for we are all of earthling measure
& magics we
are carrying

SELF PORTRAIT PRETENDING TO BE A STONE
STATUE OF MYSELF [after Jimmie Durham]

it matters that verse is imperfect
because perfection is an illusion
& crystalline is an estate

WOMAN BY THE SEA [after Cecil Higgs]

"the open song of the ones who are supposed to be silent"
—Stefano Harney & Fred Moten

my dress still aches
as my toes rest
in pebbled shallows
of wispy sea-ash

as goose flesh
my handheld
limbs and torso
with each stuttering
each tidal
in breathing mammal

as I shake loose
the sea-dew
my wetted hair drags
most severely

called forth
as starlight's
awakened foam
and ever after
moon-spun
lady-like
and bratty

then as I imp-flap the galactic
words fall away
and into sound
and into spatial
rivulets

sing-songs, star-wept
as when our babies
and our selves crest
like the birthing
like the dying
of the elements
& of the motions
of our stars

so many sea-stars
as we squirrel
ourselves to sleep
while the winds pour
past our stick
& nylon temp'ral

& the moon so bright
& clear
is like an auntie's
graceful wink
for it precedes us
& lights the way

LYNX BOA (SELF-PORTRAIT)
[after Tove Jansson]

these days are brave & generous
these times are rich & apt

& of our bilocation
in your pocket cathedral
& in mine, & of all
the evening grasses

& the hearing-masques
of the avant-gardes
contain the seeds of
their relinquishing

as we learn plants names
& as the earth aches
her heroes continents
& discontents
awash in tides

as it is actually
time to go
in the fealty
& in the promise

of all the evening grasses

MIRANDA—THE TEMPEST
[after John William Waterhouse]

in maps of the sea-rug
please tell me things
say things to me
flooding & gently
& through this sea-lace
hear me please
& kindly, in the resurrection
of our sea-hut
in relinquishing our sins
& our visions herald wounds then
& of all our kin
these seasons
so very long and many
in mending
and on-sea

Easter 2015

Book Six
The Mantle (adornment [Obs.])

adornment [Obs.]

bees, dresses, maps
of heaven's alcove
at starlight's priory
a little circle of animals
singing star-songs
for we are not waylaid
are gentle
as the worlds tilt
toward dissolution
star-flecked, star-fleshed,
& unalone

contextual

offered in the heart of the goddess, which includes all gods
and brings, in the plazas as well as in the alleys, the sea-
drifts & the parlors, of all the cities of the twelfth dimension,
as we bow into this flood, the tender dissolutions, the
transparencies of the universal selfy, adornment [Obs.], the
irremarkable qualities of the gentry, as into every sea-hole, as
we are all aristocrat, & worker, & as joy, et clamor, it is done

penny harbor

in the cove affect of the lake-snow, in this tiny city,
we are not unallowed, made vast, come whole

and pleasing herself is the star-dark is the sea-bright is the
sun-flecked lass of new heaven

all the steadying means of language
& architecture
& then
unbound

at blackpool rock
in summertide

the little red along the sea-wall
my collection of birds & Marys
awash then in their very
porousness

& now & as
our veins sprout roses, apples,
everything

ASCENSION

pine, pine hollow, ash
pine, pine hollow,
ash & center, holler
& begin

IN JUNIPER, LIKE CORAL

in juniper, like coral
as the bees hum
as our cells hum
as we cultivate
our feral hopes

PARFUM

as the bees graze
toward eternity
this light in pouring
hard & fast
engentles

FEALTY

to rescind my exposition
to collapse into your arms

Book Seven
pocket cathedral

shrine # fatigue

gadget # fatigue

[let us weep // odes]

be tender to yourself

yeux

in our big eyes the city bankrupt
never to fascinate
our docile cars, & purses, mirrors
so pretty ultra, ultra

as these austerities, of eternities
all sterile lengthen,
indefinite as prose,
fierce monuments ajar
in deviance & drone
the bluey dance, swan-white
& moated

in tour after tour after tour
in blanche, & reel,
displacing extraproper
as the sphinx

after Charles Baudelaire

ark

pebbles mark the footpaths
awash in the tears of the gods
as sunlight pours & makes me
from these shell-ish seas
the skies apace with creation
& with tool, of the depths
of earth I will recall
our mother sea-saw,
geraniums like a kind procedure,
girl inventors, chance & melody

rib

while you field no generosity
the skies collapse
the clouds unhook themselves
& head home

trio

in homely joys
with mythos streaming
& our putter-play

punk couch

as we await
the discoveries
of centaurs

in votaries
& plenum

as the angels clamor
& the gods collect

in words & hours
variety

as a bee sows
toward the dawn

for Paul Jackson

scull

as mother nursed you
in song & dream

in native mother whatsay
as toward root & phrase

slate

as solar cubes
psyche attends itself
in silence   of mercy

after Edmund Spenser

funk heap

as in the late echoic
& of pine
& ash
& cloak

thresholden anchoret
even as birds
fret & groom
approach the shore

minerva

a peer/see drop/or reckoned
a penny seer/an otis stage
muse & valence/house & song
of our chalk veins/& alkaline phrasings
of our material/reclamation

Book Eight
Translucency

[sea-rocket]

Non tibi sit grave dicere mater ave.

*Vierge amiable, obtenez-moi la grace de partager les joies de votre
fils par la pratique de la simplicite.*

our lady of the honey bees,
west-oak & tidal
please help to absolve & rectify
my errors & my failings, by the lean-to,
in the shack & of the waters—
kindly guide & kindly please do
witness as I carry—
through—

as in our tidy creche grove
oh lady of this beach curfew,
& of our surveyed tides,
oh lady of our common snakes,
whipsnake & coastal scrub,
kind lady of our native oaks, deer-kin,
stick-lake & droughty—
arrived in stems & yellowbill—
as water drains & pelican
dear lady of hopes immensities,
california sister—in mourning
cloak, & alder—little
cabbage whites, &
hairstreak, be it mended,
every—thing—

for in this pipevine swallowtail
we pour our dreams our methods
like shallows to the seas

& our children skip & bathe here,
sunlight velveteen & remnant
then leads us to our songs,
widespread in grasslands,
our ladies of expansive views,
killdeer & sanderling, as a true flock
steadies its way across a mudflat—
such skunks & amphibians, sweet raptors,
winged girls, as a tiny frog's hand lingers
on a rock, our native mother whatsay,
our dreams & champions,
as into blue, purple, or yellow—
showing, also, as lady & poppy,
in common disrupted soils,
attended by bees & beetles
as of your creche hands
the bright days the rich nights carry us,
wild elementals, the shorelines & the seas,
as all mothers of the pacific rim,
as all the parents of all the worlds,
rise en-chanting for their broods & for each others
for we are made of dark & salt
of waterlight, of care of care
of care

song-sparrows, mockingbirds, & jays,
unsubtle squirrels & their cousins—
the house sprites—as into the hollows
of humanbuilt, they furrow, they
nest & cry & mate

of maps & cathedrals
the moon in the daylight

the suns at night
litter & sea, sea-rocket
so feral & so stone
stone memoir, heap

& oh
oh holy wherewithals
as we are unalone

we're curled up in an atmosphere,
present & account—
glass ornaments with recumbent deer—
& we of this gorgon library
found on stones & dolmens, & humane—
as in the cork rock & the cypress,
as of the palm & mend,
as with the red & pine

aye ladies as we all, & gentling the men—
oh lady, our lady—
in the hollows of the safe sweet night
in the calm of the fog-dawn
& the cool-dawn, & the plain

my adornment so obscured now
as I weave

oh riverlight, as
venus amid the palms
or as the birth of mary
in nest & evocation
oh riverlight, as
as

[translucency]

in these places
our outer body coverings
refract such light

to inhabit & to mend them
our houses flood with stuff

dig deep, creatures
it is a naked moon
& swanny

the imprint of the stone coursing
then fiercely unfolding
we are fire, pitted
a lot of dancing light

our minds crown each other
as our bodies dissolve
our ideas

in these soft measures
after the fullness
of the moon

as in the heart's trench
& of the birds league
to the seas

such delinquent joy, dwelling-field
this bright & stunning leap
is, after all, not so very daring
the hundred eyes of your face,

and neck, and paws
were ever obvious to me when I
my own unglued

as in the deep sleeps
of the newly born
and of all our living

it is our bright fate, dwelt
in the clinging goldens of our sun
as we pasted its echoes to our lids

clarion,
in the fargardens
are we

by the bitter light
in the sorrow light

and then
by the true, for

here is our cardinal signature
now is our languageless phrase

little tidals, unvoiced
this herald loom of ash, & plaster,
cement, & earth, unvarnished

in solemn arms
betreuthe shorn phrases
of coursing stone
along love's vast relief

& swanny
it is a naked moon

[grazed]

touched & grazed
by the sun
the pools of light &
the pools of texture

its nourishments, its actions
of our own becoming

Poems, and lines, and phrases, from this book have appeared in *American Poetry Review, Chicago Review, Delirious Hem, Dusie Advent 2016, Eleven Eleven, Entropy, Journal of Radical Light, Litmus* (UK), *Newport Life, Puerto del Sol,* and *Women Poets Wearing Sweatpants,* as well as in the Dusie kollektiv chapbook *Novitiate: a penny posy* (2014). Book Three, *Holocene,* appeared as a chapbook from a+bend press in 2016.

Penny also exists in another iteration at pennymarvel.tumblr.com.

The italicized phrases in Book One are from C.S. Lewis' *Narnia* series & those in "[sea-rocket]" of Book Eight are from *The Little Book of Mary* by Christine Barrely.

My heartfelt thanks to Paula Gunn Allen, Susana Gardner, Holly Schneider, and Jill Stengel for, each in her own way, making space in the world for this book; and also to Lyn Hejinian and everyone at Poets in Need for the Leslie Scalapino Memorial Award which carried me toward its completion.

My sweetest blessings and gratitude to Arielle Guy, Yolanda Baber Rokeach, Sarah Anne Cox, Dana Teen Lomax, Kelley Wheeler-Nelson, Carol Treadwell, Aya Rokeach, Elly Rokeach, Neave Higgins, Margaret Treadwell Minnick, and especially my daughters, Ivy Rae Jackson and Gemma Jean Jackson, for the sanctuary at belpine. —ET

Elizabeth Treadwell's previous full-length collections of poetry are *Cornstarch Figurine* and *Virginia or the mud-flap girl* from Dusie; *Chantry* and *wardolly* from Chax; *LILYFOIL + 3* from O Books; *Birds & Fancies* from Shearsman; and *Posy: a charm almanack & atlas* from Lark.

A selection from these appears in *Out of Everywhere 2: Linguistically Innovative Poetry by Women in North America & the UK* (Reality Street, 2015).

Her current projects include *Secret Mint*, essays, and *Starlit*, poems.

pennymarvel.tumblr.com
instagram.com/vivian_rialto
elizabethtreadwell.com

SIE

DU

www.ingramcontent.com/pod-product-compliance
Lightning Source LLC
Chambersburg PA
CBHW021328060726
47591CB00006B/1923